OXFORD
UNIVERSITY PRESS

Oxford International Primary History

Workbook

Helen Crawford

2

Oxford International Primary for enquiring minds

OXFORD

OXFORD
UNIVERSITY PRESS

Great Clarendon Street, Oxford, OX2 6DP, United Kingdom

Oxford University Press is a department of the University of Oxford. It furthers the University's objective of excellence in research, scholarship, and education by publishing worldwide. Oxford is a registered trade mark of Oxford University Press in the UK and in certain other countries.

British Library Cataloguing in Publication Data
Data available

ISBN: 978-0-19-841816-0

5 7 9 10 8 6 4

Paper used in the production of this book is a natural, recyclable product made from wood grown in sustainable forests. The manufacturing process conforms to the environmental regulations of the country of origin.

Printed in Great Britain by Bell and Bain Ltd, Glasgow

Acknowledgements

Cover illustration: Carlo Molinari

Illustrations: Aptara

Photos: Left to Right: p5: Evikka/Shutterstock; **p5:** Mickey Mouse toy made by Dean's, English, 1930's (velvet)/Private Collection/Photo © Bonhams, London, UK/Bridgeman Images; **p5:** DEA / A. DAGLI ORTI /Getty; **p5:** INTERFOTO/Alamy; **p5:** Science & Society Picture Library/Getty; **p5:** Nieuwland Photography/Shutterstock; **p8:** Evikka/Shutterstock; **p10 (T), p11 (TL) & p11 (ML):** DEA/A. JEMOLO/Getty; **p10 (M), p11 (TR) & p11 (BL):** Caroline P. Digonis/Alamy; **p10 (B), p11 (MR) & p11 (BR):** Beepstock/Alamy; **p13 (T):** INTERFOTO/TV-yesterday/Mary Evans; **p13 (TM):** Adrian Candela/Shutterstock; **p13 (BM):** Rob Byron/Shutterstock; **p13 (B):** Keystone-France/Getty; **p14:** Bettmann/Getty; **p33:** Wilbur Wright (1867-1912) in his 'flyer', before 1914 (colour litho), Pousthomis, Leon (1881-1916)/Musee de la Ville de Paris, Musee Carnavalet, Paris, France/Archives Charmet/Bridgeman Images; **p37 (L):** Steve Mann/Shutterstock; **p37 (R):** Steve Mann/Shutterstock; **p41:** The cosmonaut Yuri Gagarin (b/w photo), Russian Photographer (20th century)/Private Collection/Bridgeman Images; **p47:** Tim Graham/Getty; **p48:** Queen Elizabeth I (1533-1603) being carried in Procession (Eliza Triumphans) c.1601 (oil on canvas), Peake, Robert (fl.1580-1626) (attr. to)/Private Collection/Bridgeman Images; **p48:** Nednapa Sopasuntorn/Shutterstock

Although we have made every effort to trace and contact all copyright holders before publication this has not been possible in all cases. If notified, the publisher will rectify any errors or omissions at the earliest opportunity.

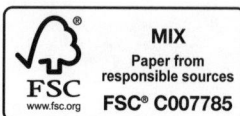

MIX
Paper from responsible sources
FSC
www.fsc.org   FSC® C007785

Contents

1 Toys and games over time

What do I already know?

Read the questions in the speech bubbles.
Tell a friend your ideas.

What are your favourite toys?

What are your favourite games?

What toys and games did your parents play with?

What toys and games did your grandparents play with?

How can we find out about the toys and games children played with in the past?

1 Look at the toys and games timeline. Colour each decade a different colour.

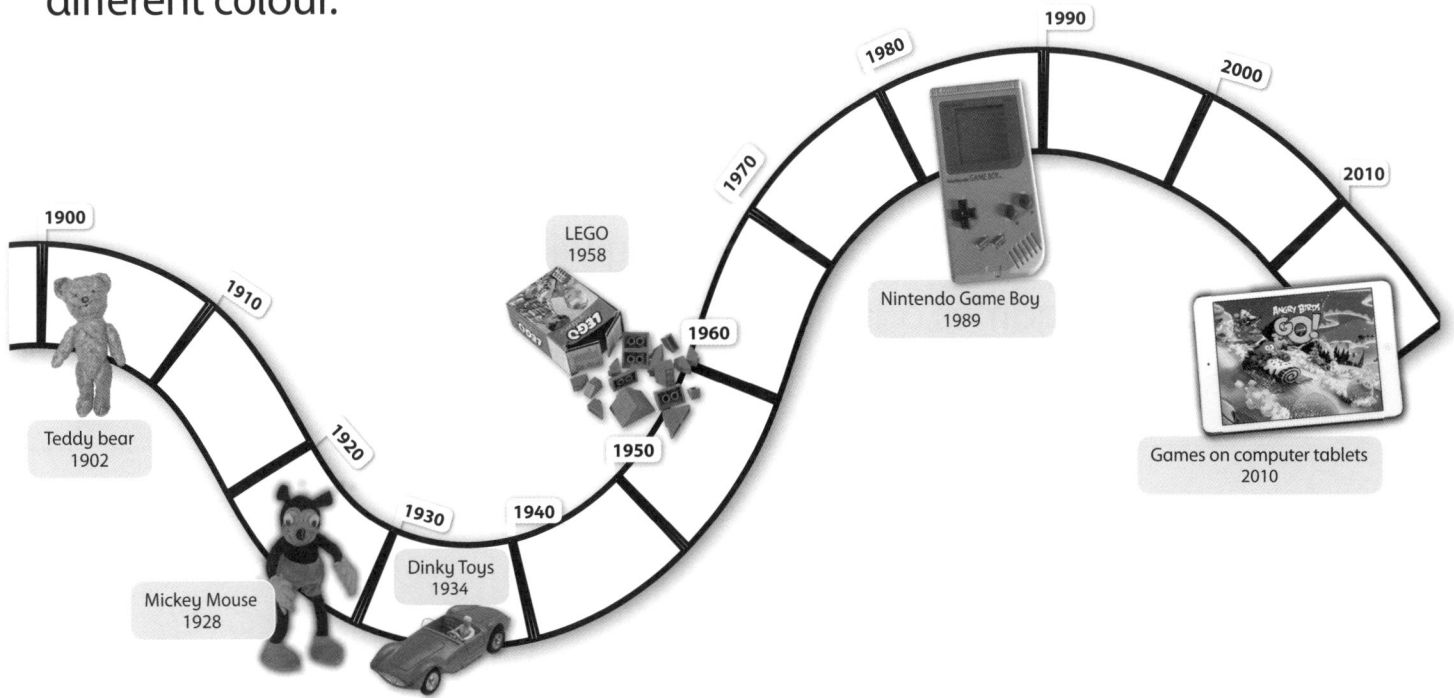

1900
1910
1920
1930
1940
1950
1960
1970
1980
1990
2000
2010

Teddy bear
1902

Mickey Mouse
1928

Dinky Toys
1934

LEGO
1958

Nintendo Game Boy
1989

Games on computer tablets
2010

2 Write the answers to the questions.

a Which is the oldest toy?

_____

b How do you know?

_____

c Which is the newest toy?

_____

d How do you know?

_____

e What different materials are these toys and games made of?

_____

What were our grandparents' favourite toys and games?

Some of the toys and games we play with today are different from the toys and games our grandparents played with. Colour the toys and games that our grandparents played with.

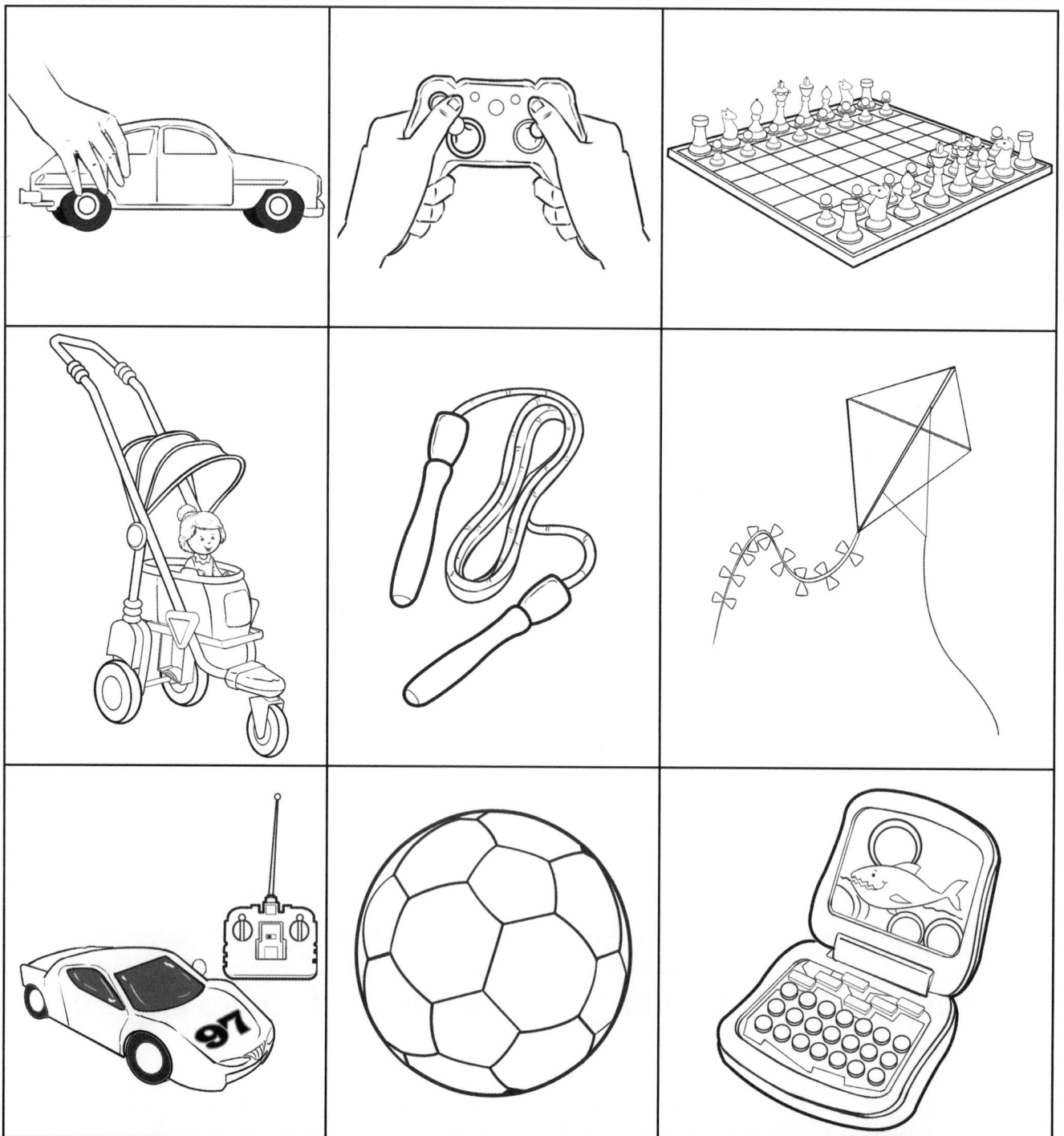

Oral history 🏠

1 Draw your favourite game or toy. Complete the sentences.

	This is a picture of my favourite toy or game. It is a
	_____
	_____.
I like it because _____
_____.

2 Talk to one of your parents or grandparents. Draw their favourite toy or game. Complete the sentences.

	This is a picture of my _____ favourite toy or game. It is a
	_____
	_____.
My _____ liked it because _____
_____.

How did the teddy bear get its name?

True or false?

Look at these sentences. Put ✓ in the box if you think the sentence is right. Put ✗ in the box if you think the sentence is wrong.

1 The first teddy bears were made in 2002. ☐

2 Theodore Roosevelt's nickname was 'Teddy'. ☐

3 Theodore Roosevelt was president of China. ☐

4 President Roosevelt went hunting with friends. ☐

5 President Roosevelt shot a small bear. ☐

Old and modern teddy bears

1 This is a modern teddy bear.
Colour the bear blue.

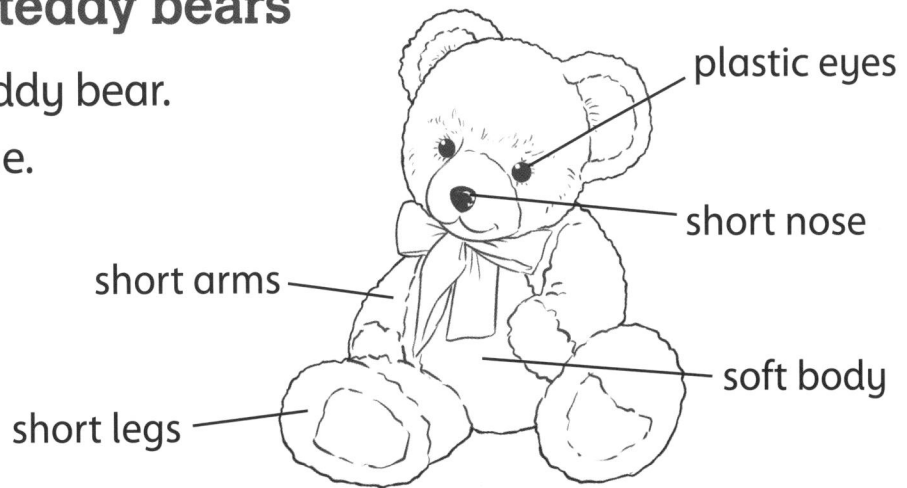

plastic eyes

short nose

short arms

soft body

short legs

2 Draw a picture of an old teddy bear. Colour the bear brown or black. Add labels to your picture. Use the words in the box to help you.

glass	hard	legs	nose
long	arms	eyes	body

Different types of doll

Read the speech bubbles. Draw a line to match each speech bubble to the correct doll.

I am 4000 years old.

I am 150 years old.

I am made of plastic.

I break easily.

I am made of wood.

I am made of china.

I am modern.

I am a paddle doll.

I was made in a factory.

How are the dolls similar?

Complete the sentences.

1 The wooden doll is similar to the china doll because

_____

_____.

2 The wooden doll is similar to the plastic doll because

_____

_____.

3 The china doll is similar to the plastic doll because

_____

_____.

1.4 Making toys move

Making toys move

At different times in the past people used different technology to make toys move.

1 Write the numbers from 1 to 4 to show the order of when people invented these toys and games.

2 Write how we make each type of toy move.

Write number (1, 2, 3 or 4)	Type of toy or game	How do we make it move?
	a toy with an electric motor	
	a clockwork toy	
	a computer game	
	a string puppet	

Then and now

Draw pictures to show what these moving toys and games look like today. Write a label for each picture.

In the past   **Today**

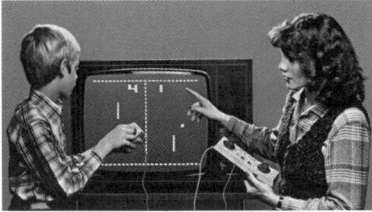

A computer game

A clockwork toy

A puppet

A toy with an electric motor

Looking at real cars

This is a picture of one of the first real cars. The car was made by Karl Benz.

Draw a picture of a modern car. Label the different parts of the car. Use the words in the box to help you.

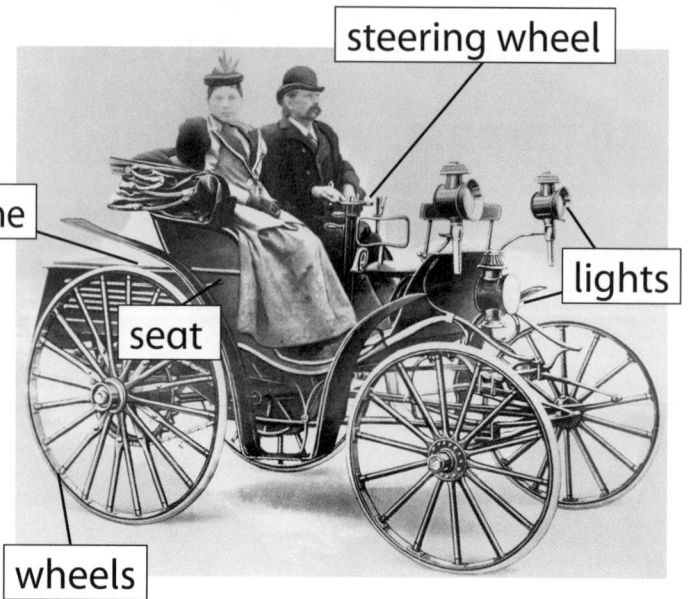

steering wheel

engine

lights

seat

wheels

wheels	lights	doors	glass
engine	roof	steering wheel	

Similar and different

Look at this old toy car and this modern toy car. Write in the table how they are similar and how they are different. Use some of the words in the box on page 14 to help you.

Write three ways the cars are similar.
1
2
3

Write three ways the cars are different.
1
2
3

Toys over time

How have toys and games changed over time?

_____

_____

_____

Challenge

Why have toys and games changed over time?

_____

_____

_____

Thinking about my learning

Learning outcome I can...	☺	😐	☹
compare old and modern toys and games.			
describe how toys and games have changed.			
explain why toys and games have changed.			
put toys and games in order on a timeline.			

Three things I have learned...

1 _____

2 _____

3 _____

My favourite activity was...

_____

My favourite fact was...

_____

I would like to know more about...

_____

What do I already know?

Read the questions in the speech bubbles.

Tell a friend your ideas.

What is a queen?

Which famous queens can you name?

What does royal mean?

What is the capital city of England?

Which continent is England in?

A timeline of the three queens

Look at the timeline. It shows the reigns of the three queens. Answer the questions.

1 In which century was Elizabeth I born?

_____

2 In which century was Victoria born?

_____

3 In which century was Elizabeth II born?

_____

4 Which queen is alive today?

_____

5 How do you know which queen is alive today?

_____

_____

Queen
Elizabeth I
1558–1603 CE

16th century

17th century

18th century

Queen
Victoria
1837–1901 CE

19th century

Queen
Elizabeth II
1952–

20th century

21st century

Who was Queen Elizabeth I?

Queen Elizabeth I

True or false?

Look at these sentences. Put ✓ in the box if you think the sentence is right. Put ✗ in the box if you think the sentence is wrong.

1 Elizabeth was born in 1533 CE. ☐

2 Elizabeth grew up in a small house. ☐

3 Elizabeth got married. ☐

4 Elizabeth loved music. ☐

5 The king of France sent ships to attack England. ☐

6 Elizabeth and the royal court liked to travel. ☐

7 Elizabeth was queen for 60 years. ☐

8 Elizabeth died in 1603. ☐

Danger at sea!

Look at these pictures. Write sentences next to each picture to tell the story of the attack by the Spanish Armada. Use the words in the box to help you.

king	Spain		battle	Elizabeth
ship	Spanish Armada		attack	1588

1 _____

_____

_____

2 _____

_____

_____

3 _____

_____

_____

4 _____

_____

_____

A long reign

1 Draw a line from each date to the correct event in my life.

| Princess Victoria was born. | 1861 |

| Victoria became queen. | 1837 |

| Victoria's husband Albert died. | 1819 |

| Queen Victoria celebrated her Diamond Jubilee. | 1901 |

| Queen Victoria died. | 1897 |

2 Write the dates from Queen Victoria's life in the correct order on the timeline.

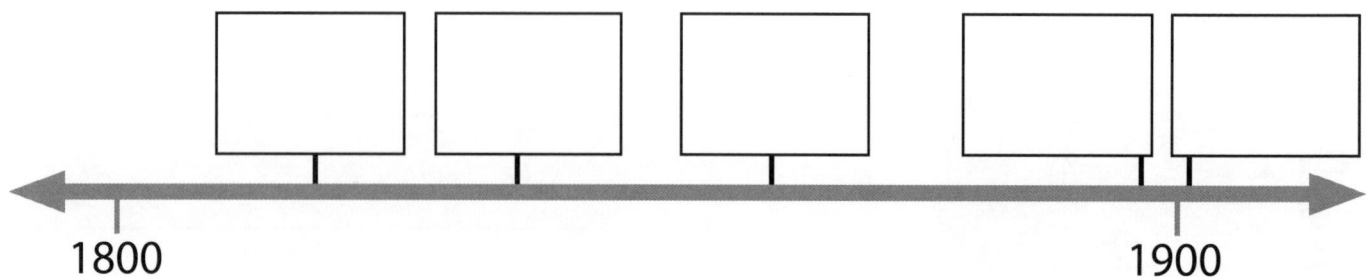

1800   1900

3 Which of the dates is in the 20th century? _____

Local history study

Queen Victoria was the ruler of the British Empire. Many places in the world are named after her. Think about where you live. Choose a place that is named after a famous person from the past. The place could be a street, a park or a building.

1 Draw a picture of the place.

2 Complete the sentences.

a The place I chose is _____.

b It is named after _____.

c This person lived in the _____ century.

d This person was important because

_____

_____

_____

A royal coronation

1 Draw a picture on this television screen of Queen Elizabeth II on her coronation day.

2 Complete the sentences. Use the words in the box.

million	television	ceremony
1952	second	

A coronation is the _____ when a person

becomes a king or a queen. Elizabeth became queen

in _____. Elizabeth's coronation was shown on

_____.

In the UK, 27 _____ people watched her

become queen. She is called Elizabeth II because she is the

_____ Queen Elizabeth.

In the news

Look at these newspaper headlines about Elizabeth II's life. Which event is each headline describing? Write a sentence for each answer.

1

20 November 1947

A Royal Marriage

_____

_____

2

21 April 1926

A New Princess

_____

_____

3

5 JUNE 2012

DIAMOND QUEEN

_____

_____

What can we learn from a portrait?

A portrait is a painting or photo of a person. A portrait is a good way to learn about people in the past. Look at these portraits. Answer the questions.

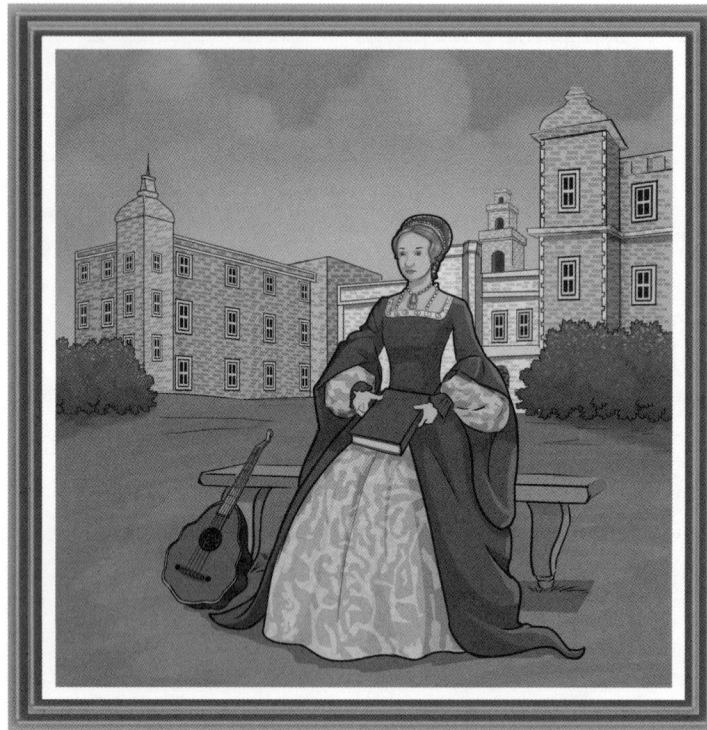

1 What can you see?

_____

_____

2 What does this portrait tell you about Queen Elizabeth I?

_____

_____

3 What can you see?

_____

_____

4 What does this portrait tell you about Queen Victoria?

_____

_____

5 What can you see?

_____

_____

6 What does this portrait tell you about Queen Elizabeth II?

_____

_____

2.5 Different times

Different times

Elizabeth I, Victoria and Elizabeth II were queens at different times. Read the sentences in the speech bubbles. Draw a line to match each sentence to the correct queen.

Electric lights lit up streets and houses.

People travelled in steam trains.

English ships sailed around the world for the first time.

The telephone was invented.

Rockets travelled into space.

The Internet connected computers all around the world.

The mobile phone was invented.

William Shakespeare wrote famous plays.

What do you think?

1 The most exciting thing about Elizabeth I's reign was

_____

because _____.

2 The most exciting thing about Victoria's reign was

_____

because _____.

3 The most exciting thing about Elizabeth II's reign was

_____

because _____.

Three queens

Complete the information for each queen.

	 Elizabeth I	 Victoria	 Elizabeth II
In which century was she born?			
Did she go to school?			
Did she get married?			
Did she have a Diamond Jubilee?			
What is one reason she is special?			

Challenge

I think _____ and _____ are the

most similar queens because _____

_____.

Thinking about my learning

Learning outcome I can...	☺	😐	☹
talk about the reigns of three English queens.			
compare three different English queens.			
compare life at different times in the past.			

Three things I have learned...

1 _____

2 _____

3 _____

My favourite activity was...

_____

My favourite fact was...

_____

I would like to know more about...

_____

What do I already know?

Read the questions in the speech bubbles.
Tell a friend your ideas.

What different types of aircraft can you name?

What is a pilot?

What is an astronaut?

Have you ever flown in an airplane?

Would you like to travel into space one day?

Look at the picture of the airplane. Answer the questions.

1 What can you see?

_____

2 What do you think this airplane is made of?

_____

3 When do you think it was made?

_____

4 How is this airplane similar to the airplanes that fly today?

_____

5 How is this airplane different from the airplanes that fly today?

_____

The first balloon flight

True or false?

Look at these sentences. Put ✓ in the box if you think the sentence is right. Put ✗ in the box if you think the sentence is wrong.

1 The Montgolfier brothers were called Joseph and Adam.

2 The brothers were from France.

3 The first balloon flight took place in 1783.

4 There was a fire inside the balloon to heat the air.

5 The balloon was made of paper and plastic.

6 The first balloon flight carried a duck, a rooster and a dog.

7 In November 1783, two men flew over the city of Paris in a balloon.

8 The two men flew for 25 hours.

Success!

The Montgolfier brothers became famous. The king of France gave the brothers a special award.

Complete this certificate to congratulate the Montgolfier brothers for the first balloon flight.

This certificate is awarded to

_____

For the success of

_____

_____

_____

_____

_____

_____

_____

_____

The Wright brothers

Complete the newspaper report about the first airplane flight.
Use the words in the box to help you.

Orville	Wright	biplane	pilot
Wilbur	Flyer	the USA	12 seconds

The Daily News

Friday 18 December 1903

Write your headline here.

On the 17th December an airplane with an engine flew in the sky for the first time.

_____

_____

Draw a picture here.

_____

_____

_____

_____

Looking at stamps

These stamps tell us about the first airplane flight. One stamp is from Liberia in Africa. The other stamp is from Romania in Europe.

1 Design your own stamp about the Wright brothers' flight.

2 Stamps often show pictures of famous people or events from the past. Can you explain why?

_____

_____

_____

Old and modern airplanes

Look at these two airplanes. Label the different parts of each airplane. Use the words in the box to help you.

engine	wings	pilot	luggage
propellers	wires	passengers	jet engine

A modern jet airplane

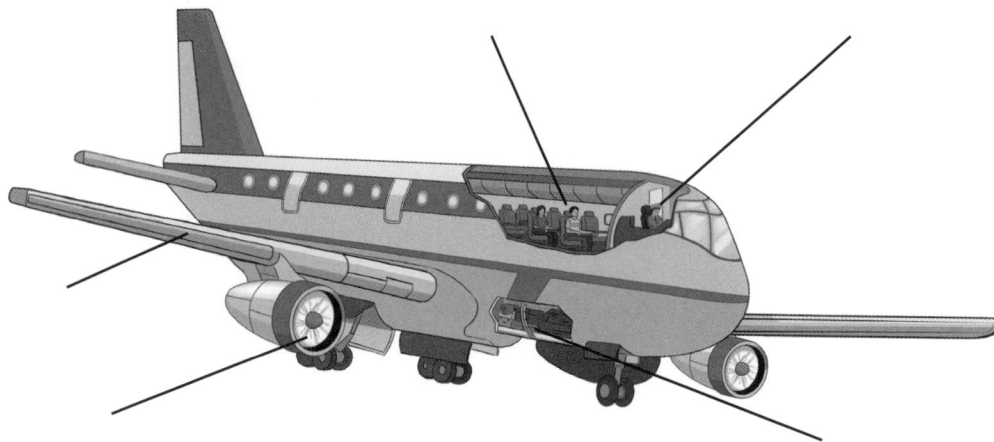

The Wright brothers' airplane, 1903

Similar and different

Write three ways in which the two airplanes are similar.	Write three ways in which the two airplanes are different.
1 2 3	1 2 3

Flying today

Talk to three people who have flown in an airplane. Ask each person the questions in the table and complete the table.

Name of person	Which airport did you fly from?	Where did you fly to?	Why did you travel to this place?

The Space Age

1 Draw a line from each date to the correct event.

| October 1957 |

Valentina Tereshkova became the first woman in space.

| November 1957 |

The first spacewalk took place.

| April 1961 |

A dog was sent into space.

| June 1963 |

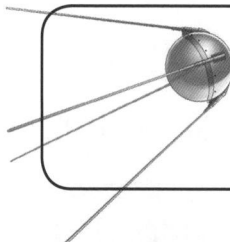

A satellite called Sputnik orbited the Earth.

| March 1965 |

Yuri Gagarin became the first man in space.

2 Which of these events do you think was the most important?

_____

3 Why?

Being an astronaut

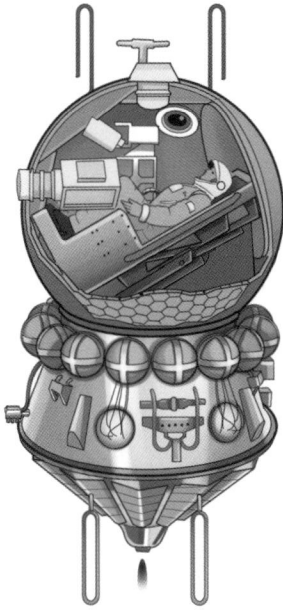

> When I orbited the Earth in a spaceship, I saw for the first time how beautiful our planet is.

Yuri Gagarin was the first astronaut to go into space. Would you have liked to be one of the first astronauts? Why? Why not?

Write some sentences to explain your ideas. Use the words in the box to help you.

astronaut	spacewalk	dangerous	brave
spacecraft	Earth	exciting	space

_____

_____

_____

_____

_____

_____

Moon landing

Look at these pictures. Write sentences to tell the story of the first moon landing. Use the words in the box to help you.

Apollo 11	Michael Collins	moon rocks	spacecraft
astronaut	Neil Armstrong	July 1969	Buzz Aldrin

That's one small step for a man, one giant leap for mankind.

Oral history 🏠

Oral history is when we talk to people about their lives in the past. Talk to an adult who remembers the first moon landing. Read the questions in the speech bubbles to help you.

> How old were you in 1969?

> Where did you live?

> Did you watch the moon landing on television?

> What do you remember about the moon landing?

> Did you read about the moon landing in a newspaper?

Complete the sentences.

1 I spoke to _____ about the moon landing.

2 In 1969 this person was _____ years old.

3 In 1969 this person lived in _____.

4 The person told me _____

_____

_____.

3 Thinking about my learning

Draw lines to match the correct dates, names and events. The first one has been done for you.

1963	Neil Armstrong	The first machine in space
1783	The Wright brothers	The first hot air balloon flight
1961	Valentina Tereshkova	The first airplane flight
1969	The Montgolfier brothers	The first person to walk on the moon
1957	Yuri Gagarin	The first woman in space
1903	Sputnik	The first man in space

Challenge

'The first pilots were braver than the first astronauts.'

Explain whether you agree or disagree with this statement.

_____

_____

_____

Thinking about my learning

Learning outcome I can...	🙂	😐	🙁
describe how air travel developed over time.			
compare old and modern airplanes.			
discuss important events in the history of air and space travel.			

Three things I have learned...

1 _____

2 _____

3 _____

My favourite activity was...

_____

My favourite fact was...

_____

I would like to know more about...

_____

Glossary

Write what each word means or draw a picture.

aircraft

astronaut

empire

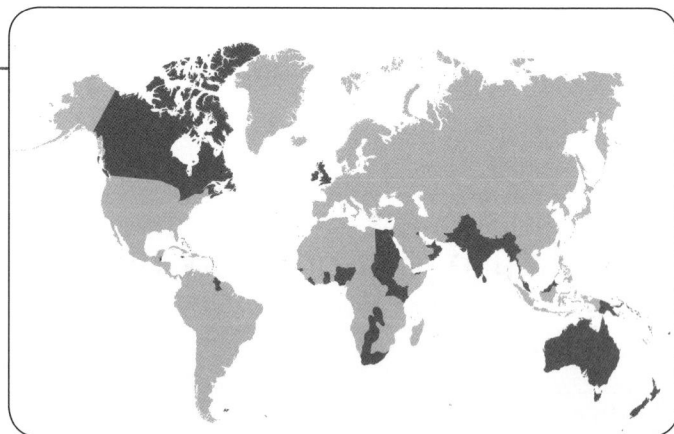

oral history

pilot

portrait

reign

royal

technology

timeline

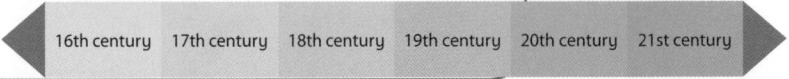

Queen Elizabeth I

Queen Victoria

Queen Elizabeth II

16th century · 17th century · 18th century · 19th century · 20th century · 21st century